Bugs and Us

FIRST EDITION
Series Editor Deborah Lock; **US Editor** Shannon Beatty; **Designer** Neetika Vilash;
Project Designer Akanksha Gupta; **Art Director** Martin Wilson;
Production Editor Sarah Isle; **Jacket Designer** Natalie Godwin;
Entomology Consultant Professor May Berenbaum, University of Illinois at Urbana-Champaign;
Reading Consultant Linda Gambrell, PhD

THIS EDITION
Editorial Management by Oriel Square
Produced for DK by WonderLab Group LLC
Jennifer Emmett, Erica Green, Kate Hale, *Founders*

Editors Grace Hill Smith, Libby Romero, Michaela Weglinski;
Photography Editors Kelley Miller, Annette Kiesow, Nicole DiMella; **Managing Editor** Rachel Houghton;
Designers Project Design Company; **Researcher** Michelle Harris; **Copy Editor** Lori Merritt;
Indexer Connie Binder; **Proofreader** Larry Shea; **Reading Specialist** Dr. Jennifer Albro;
Curriculum Specialist Elaine Larson

Published in the United States by DK Publishing
1745 Broadway, 20th Floor, New York, NY 10019

Copyright © 2023 Dorling Kindersley Limited
DK, a Division of Penguin Random House LLC
23 24 25 26 10 9 8 7 6 5 4 3 2 1
001-333923-June/2023

All rights reserved.

Without limiting the rights under the copyright reserved above, no part of this publication may be reproduced, stored in or introduced into a retrieval system, or transmitted, in any form, or by any means (electronic, mechanical, photocopying, recording, or otherwise), without the prior written permission of the copyright owner.
Published in Great Britain by Dorling Kindersley Limited

A catalog record for this book
is available from the Library of Congress.
HC ISBN: 978-0-7440-7250-1
PB ISBN: 978-0-7440-7251-8

DK books are available at special discounts when purchased in bulk for sales promotions, premiums, fundraising, or educational use. For details, contact: DK Publishing Special Markets,
1745 Broadway, 20th Floor, New York, NY 10019
SpecialSales@dk.com

Printed and bound in China

The publisher would like to thank the following for their kind permission to reproduce their images:
a=above; c=center; b=below; l=left; r=right; t=top; b/g=background
Dreamstime.com: Ecophoto 21br, Karelgallas 15bl; **Getty Images:** RooM / dikkyoesin1 19tr
Cover images: *Front:* **Shutterstock.com:** revers c

All other images © Dorling Kindersley
For more information see: www.dkimages.com

For the curious
www.dk.com

Level 2

Bugs and Us

Patricia J. Murphy

Contents

6	Insects Can Bug Us
8	Insects as Helpers
14	Pest Controllers
22	Planet Protectors

28 Helping Bugs Helps Us
30 Glossary
31 Index
32 Quiz

Insects Can Bug Us

Buzz.

Buzz.

Scratch.
Scratch.

Insects can really bug us!

Some grasshopper species can destroy crops.

Many insects buzz
in our ears.
Some bite or sting us.
Others can hurt our crops,
wreck our picnics—
and make people sick!

Insects as Helpers

You might ask, "Who needs insects?" The answer is, everybody does!

Most insects do more good than bad. In fact, many insects help us grow the food we need to survive!

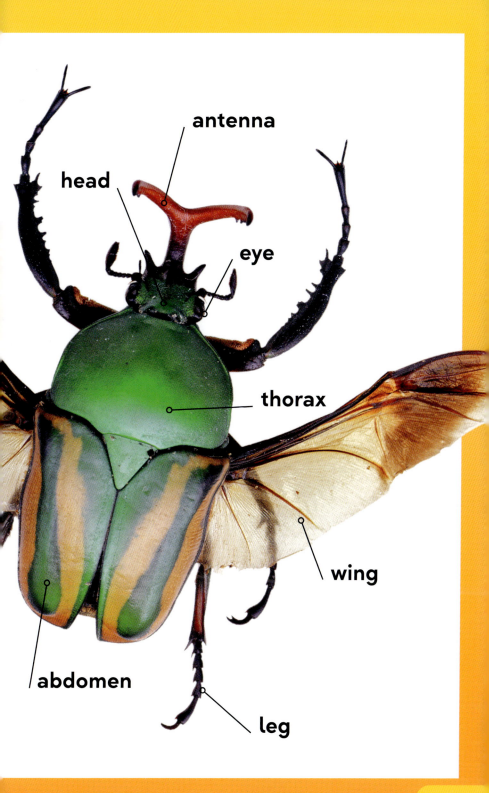

Bees, wasps, flies, beetles, and butterflies are great pollinators. They buzz from flower to flower, spreading pollen. Pollen helps flowers make seeds.

pollen

Some of these seeds grow into many of the fruits, vegetables, and foods we eat.

Honey bees drink nectar from flowers and turn it into honey. They build honeycomb with beeswax to store both honey and pollen.

nectar

Many people and animals love the taste of honey. Beeswax is used to make candles and other things.

13

Pest Controllers

Some insects eat other insects! This keeps insect groups from getting too big.

This praying mantis eats a bee. They have also been known to eat moths, beetles, crickets, and even small birds!

Praying mantises and green lacewings feast on insects, large and small. Dragonflies eat 300 to 400 mosquitoes a day. But, soon, other animal friends will eat them!

A bee-eater about to catch a wasp

Ladybugs and their larvae are farmers' best friends. They eat teeny crop-eating insects called aphids.

Ladybugs can't get
enough of them!
Many farmers use ladybugs
instead of sprays
that can harm
other living things.

larva

Some ants protect plants from harm. They bite and sting plant-eating insects and other animals. They act like bodyguards for their plant pals. Other ants move seeds and soil around so that new plants can grow.

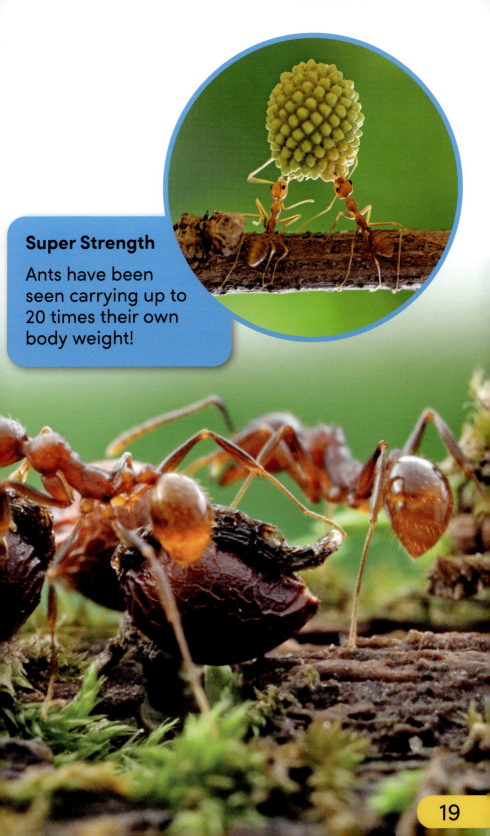

Super Strength

Ants have been seen carrying up to 20 times their own body weight!

spider

Spiders help keep our homes and gardens safe from pests.
They catch and collect insects in their wonderful webs. These silky, sticky webs are beautiful to look at.

Not Quite Insects

Spiders are not true insects. They are in the same family as daddy longlegs, scorpions, and ticks.

Planet Protectors

Some insects do nature's dirty work. Dung beetles eat the waste of animals.

Termites feed on rotting wood.
Flies and carrion beetles
feed on dead animals.
These insects rid the Earth
of waste—and help recycle it.

Light Up the Night

Fireflies are fun to watch, but they need darkness to survive. Make sure to turn off outdoor lights when they aren't needed so these bugs can keep lighting up the night.

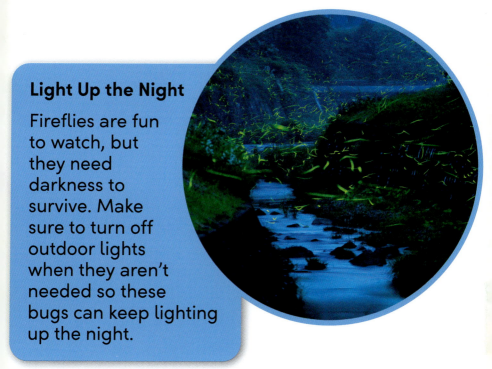

Many insects add beauty to our world.
Butterflies flash bright colors and patterns as they flutter by.
Flickering fireflies light up the night sky.
Chirping crickets sing simple songs.

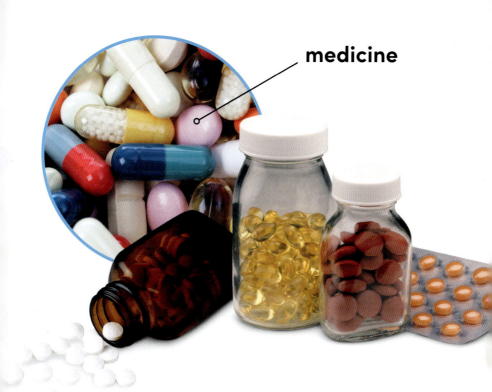

medicine

Other insects help scientists. Fruit flies and flour beetles show scientists how animals change as they grow. Mayflies and stoneflies tell them if streams are clean. Beetles and butterflies help them make new medicines that could save people's lives.

Helping Bugs Helps Us

Insects help us in many ways.
We can help them, too.
We can plant flowers
and grow plants.
We can learn
how to save their homes.
We can enjoy them—
and let them live.

Buzz.

Buzz.

Buzz.

Antenna
One of a pair of thin, movable organs on an insect's head

Butterfly
An insect with colorful scales on its wings and a long tongue called a proboscis [pro-BAS-kiss]

Larva
An insect during the early stages of its life

Medicine
A drug used to treat or prevent diseases

Nectar
The sugary-sweet liquid from a flower

Pollen
A tiny grain that helps flowers make new seeds

Spider
An animal with a short abdomen, fangs, and an organ that can make threads of silk

Thorax
The middle part of an insect's body between its neck and abdomen

Index

abdomen 9
antenna 9
ants 18–19
aphids 16
bees 10, 13, 14
beetles 10, 14, 22, 23, 27
butterflies 10, 25, 27
carrion beetles 23
crickets 14, 25
dragonflies 15
dung beetles 22
eye 9

fireflies 25
flies 10, 23
flour beetles 27
fruit flies 27
grasshoppers 7
green lacewings 15
head 9
honey 13
ladybugs 16–17
larvae 16, 17
leg 9
mayflies 27
mosquitoes 15

moths 14
nectar 13
pest controllers 14–21
pollen 10, 13
praying mantises 14, 15
spiders 20, 21
stoneflies 27
termites 23
thorax 9
wasps 10, 15
wing 9

Quiz

Answer the questions to see what you have learned. Check your answers in the key below.

1. How do pollinators help us grow fruits and vegetables?
2. How many mosquitoes do dragonflies eat per day?
3. What are the crop-eating insects that ladybugs eat?
4. Why are dung beetles, termites, and flies important?
5. What are some of the insects that can help scientists make new medicines?

1. By spreading pollen from flower to flower 2. 300 to 400 mosquitoes 3. Aphids 4. They help rid the Earth of waste 5. Beetles and butterflies